This delightfully simple version retells some of the
stories about Moses's early life. It will appeal
to all young listeners and early readers.
The text is based on the first three chapters of Exodus.

Titles in Series S846
The First Christmas
*Noah's Ark
*Moses
*Joseph
*David
*Daniel
*These titles are available as a Gift Box set.

LADYBIRD BOOKS, INC.
Lewiston, Maine 04240 U.S.A.
© LADYBIRD BOOKS LTD MCMLXXXV
Loughborough, Leicestershire, England
© Illustrations LYNN N. GRUNDY MCMLXXXV

Printed in England

Moses

written by HY MURDOCK
illustrated by LYNN N. GRUNDY

Ladybird Books

A long time ago, Egypt was the land of the Egyptians, but many Israelites also lived there.

The leader of Egypt was called the Pharaoh, and he was worried about so many Israelites living in his country. He had been very unkind to them and made them work hard, as slaves.

Each year more and more Israelite babies were born in Egypt.

Pharaoh was frightened that one day the Israelites would join his enemies and fight against the Egyptian people. He wanted to kill some of the Israelite babies.

Pharaoh called the midwives to him. These women helped at the birth of a baby. He told them that they must kill all the baby boys.

The midwives knew that this would make God angry, so they didn't do what they were told. Then Pharaoh told his people that every baby boy should be thrown into the river. One Israelite family had a baby son. The mother hid him so that he would not be taken and thrown into the river.

When the baby was three months old, his mother decided to make a cradle for him so that she could hide her son away from her house.

She wove the leaves of bulrushes into a basket shape and filled the cracks with tar and mud so that it would float on water.

Then she put the baby in this cradle and hid it in the reeds growing at the edge of the river. The mother told the boy's sister, Miriam, to go and hide near the river and watch over the baby.

One day Pharaoh's daughter was walking by
the side of the river. She saw the cradle and
sent her maid to fetch it. When she looked
inside, she saw a baby crying and she felt
sorry for him.

She knew the baby was an Israelite boy, but
she wanted to keep him.

Miriam came out from her hiding place and asked if Pharaoh's daughter wanted a nurse to look after the child. When she said yes, Miriam went to fetch her mother to be the nurse.

Soon the boy was big enough to go and live at
the palace with Pharaoh's daughter. She
called him Moses because she had found him
in the water and that's what the name meant.

Moses grew into a man. He had always known that he was an Israelite, and he was unhappy that his people were slaves. One day he saw an Egyptian hitting an Israelite, and he went to help. Moses killed the Egyptian. Pharaoh found out about this and wanted to kill Moses.

Moses was frightened and ran away to a place called Midian. He was resting by a well when the daughters of a priest came to get water for their sheep. Some shepherds tried to stop the girls, but Moses helped them.

When they got home, they told their father what had happened.

Their father said that they should go back and ask Moses to come to the house to eat with them.

After that Moses stayed at their house. He married one of the girls and worked for her father as a shepherd.

While he was looking after the sheep, Moses saw a bush on fire. He went nearer and saw that the flames were not burning the bush. A voice spoke to him. It seemed to be coming from the middle of the bush.

It was God's voice, and Moses was frightened and wouldn't look.

God told Moses that he knew how unhappy the Israelites were in Egypt. God wanted Moses to show the Israelites the way to a new and better land. Moses didn't think that the Israelites would listen to him. He thought that they wouldn't believe that God had spoken to him. But God promised to help him.

God told Moses that he must go back and see
the new Pharaoh and ask him to let the
Israelites leave Egypt. So Moses did as God
had asked, but it was a long, long time before
the Pharaoh said yes.

And that is another story.